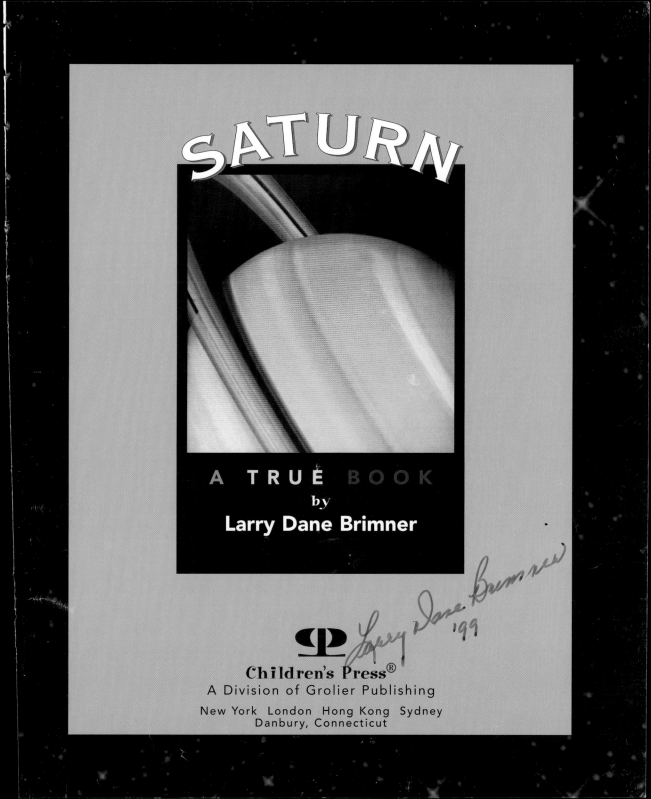

SATURN

A TRUE BOOK

by

Larry Dane Brimner

Children's Press®

A Division of Grolier Publishing

New York London Hong Kong Sydney
Danbury, Connecticut

Saturn's rings

Subject Consultant
Peter Goodwin
*Science Department Chairman
Kent School, Kent, CT*

Reading Consultant
Linda Cornwell
*Learning Resource Consultant
Indiana Department
of Education*

Author's note:
*The author wishes to thank
Maria Schuchardt of the
University of Arizona's
Lunar Planetary Lab for
answering questions and
confirming information.*

Author's dedication:
For the Hydesville Wildcats

Visit Children's Press® on the
Internet at:
http://publishing.grolier.com

Enjoy!

Larry Dane Brimner

Library of Congress Cataloging-in-Publication Data

Brimner, Larry Dane.
    Saturn / by Larry Dane Brimner.
        p.   cm. — (A true book)
    Includes bibliographical references and index.
    Summary: Examines the physical characteristics and conditions of
Saturn, describing its position in relation to the sun and other planets and
surveying humanity's attempts to penetrate its mysteries.
    ISBN 0-516-21154-4 (lib. bdg.)   0-516-26501-6 (pbk.)
    1. Saturn (Planet)—Juvenile literature. [1. Saturn (Planet)] I. Title.
II. Series.
QB671.B75 1998
523.46—dc21   98-14006
                                                                            CIP
                                                                            AC

GROLIER
PUBLISHING

Contents

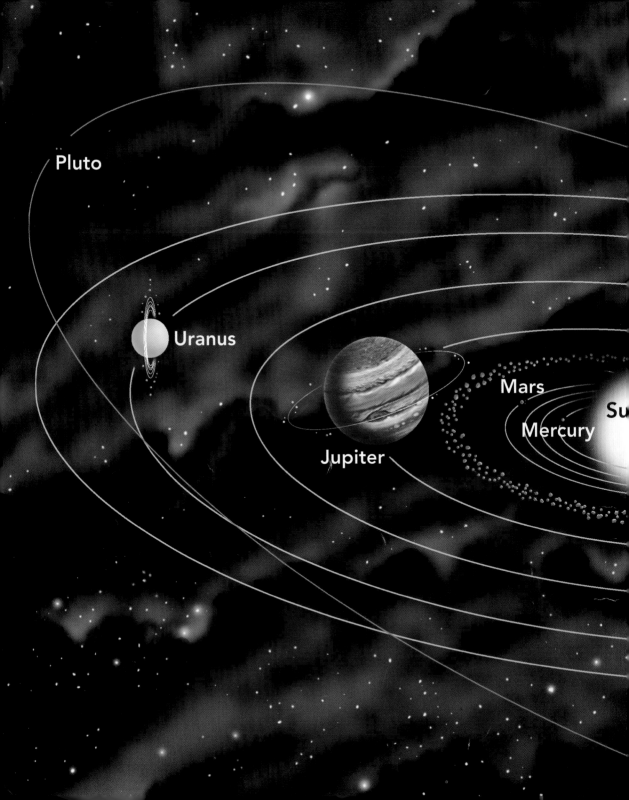

The Solar System

Venus

Earth

Moon

Asteroid Belt

Saturn

Neptune

A Planet with Ears

Saturn is one of nine planets that travel around the Sun. Their paths around the Sun are called orbits. The planets, along with other objects that orbit the Sun, make up the solar system. The four planets closest to the Sun are called the inner planets. The other

Saturn is one of the
outer planets.

five are called the outer planets. Saturn is one of the outer planets. It is the sixth planet from the Sun.

In 1610, the Italian scientist Galileo Galilei (1564–1642) looked at Saturn through his telescope. He was puzzled by what he saw. Saturn looked different from any of the other planets. "Saturn has ears," he wrote, describing bulges on either side of the planet. Today we know that those "ears" are

Galileo studied
the solar system,
including Saturn.

really rings that circle the
planet. Saturn's rings make
this planet one of the most
beautiful in the solar system.

A Gas Giant

Saturn is the second-largest planet in the solar system. It is a "gas giant" like Jupiter, Uranus, and Neptune. These planets are mostly whirling bodies of gas.

The gases that surround a planet make up its atmosphere. Saturn's atmosphere

Saturn's atmosphere is made up of whirling gases.

is mainly hydrogen and helium. You could not breathe Saturn's atmosphere because it has no oxygen and contains gases that are poisonous to people.

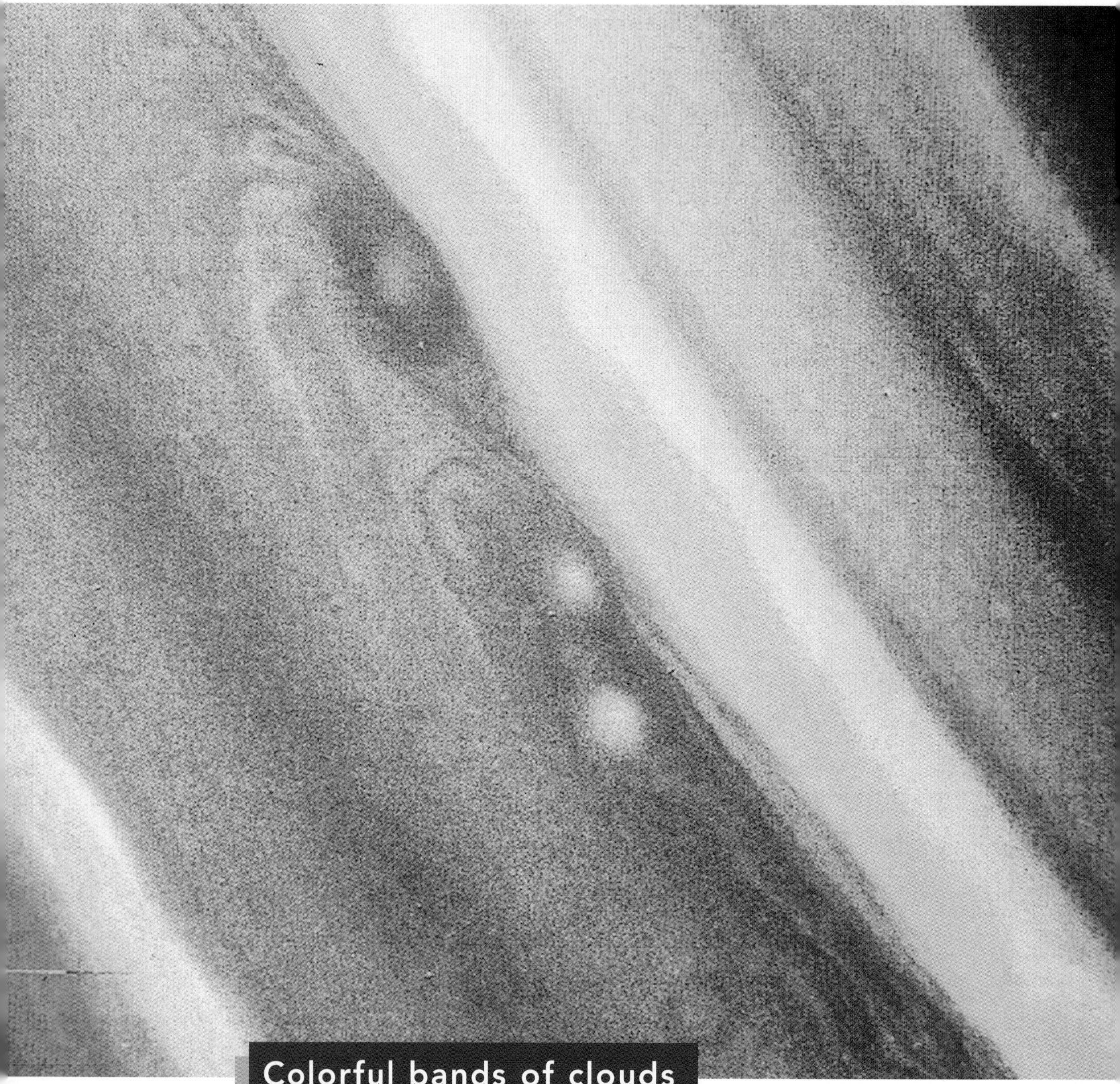

Colorful bands of clouds surround the planet. Astronomers have not yet seen below them.

The atmosphere around Saturn is very cold. Usually, gases are invisible, but Saturn's cold temperatures cause the gases in the atmosphere to freeze into crystals. The crystals make up the swirling bands of clouds that circle the planet. So scientists are actually looking at clouds when they look at Saturn through their telescopes. They have never really seen Saturn's surface.

What lies beneath Saturn's clouds? Saturn doesn't have a solid surface like Earth does. Scientists think that deep within the clouds, Saturn's atmosphere changes from a gas into a liquid. This liquid—called "liquid hydrogen"—forms Saturn's "surface." You would not be able to walk or play on it the way you can on Earth's surface.

At the very center of Saturn is a rocky core. Scientists think this rocky core is about the same size as Earth.

A rocky core can be found in the center of Saturn. It is about the same size as Earth.

On the Move

The farther a planet is from the Sun, the longer its year—or the time it takes to make its orbit around the Sun. Earth's journey takes 365 days, or one Earth-year. But Saturn is much farther away at an average distance of 885 million miles (1.4 billion kilometers). So its

Saturn is not perfectly round. Its sides seem to bulge.

journey takes much longer—29.5 Earth-years to complete one orbit.

Saturn is wider in one direction than it is in the other. Across the middle, or equator, Saturn measures 74,853 miles

(120,500 km). But from pole to pole, it measures 67,520 miles (108,700 km). Why is Saturn flattened at the poles?

Saturn is wider at the equator because of its rotation. While each planet orbits the Sun, it also spins, or rotates, on its axis—an imaginary line running from pole to pole. It is daytime on the side of the planet that faces the Sun and nighttime on the side that is in darkness. One day equals one

The Sun only lights up half of Saturn at a time.

full rotation. Saturn's day is only 10 hours and 39 minutes long. Compare this to Earth's day, which is 24 hours long. Saturn spins much faster than

Earth does. This rapid rotation causes it to bulge at its equator.

How does this happen? Imagine you are standing on a merry-go-round. As the merry-go-round's speed increases, you may feel as though you are being pulled outward. The same thing happens to Saturn. It spins so rapidly that the gases and liquids that make up the planet are pulled outward along its equator.

Saturn's Rings

The "ears" Galileo saw confused scientists at first. Some thought Saturn and its ears were three separate planets. But by 1656, astronomers were using better telescopes than those Galileo used. They were able to get a better look at objects in the night

By the mid-1600s,
scientists realized
that Saturn's "ears"
were really rings
around the planet.

sky, including Saturn. So Dutch astronomer Christiaan Huygens (1629–1695) came up with a new idea to explain Saturn's ears. He said there was a ring around Saturn.

In 1675, French astronomer Giovanni Cassini (1625–1712) noticed something else—a dark band in Saturn's ring. He realized the band was an opening separating two rings. Then in 1837, German astronomer Johann Encke (1791–1865) saw

Astronomer Cassini observed a dark band separating Saturn's rings.

another division. It was clear that Saturn's ears were really several rings around the planet.

What's in a Ring?

Saturn's rings are made up mainly of particles of water ice. They may also contain dust and rock. Information from the *Voyager* spacecraft told us that the particles vary greatly in size. Some are as small as pebbles. Others are bigger than a bus! Saturn's rings span 155,000 miles (250,000 km) or more from edge to edge, but they are no more than 1 mile (1.6 km) thick.

Learning More

In the late 1950s, the United States and the Soviet Union (now Russia) began to send probes, or spacecraft, into space. These probes were like small scientific laboratories. They took photographs and did experiments. Then they sent the information back to

In 1979, *Pioneer 11* took this first close-up look at Saturn.

Earth. Most of what we know about Saturn came from probes flying close to the planet.

Pioneer 11 gave us the first close-up look at Saturn's rings. It was launched in 1973 and reached Saturn in 1979. Until then, most scientists believed that Saturn had four or five major rings. *Pioneer 11* discovered two new rings. It also discovered swirls in Saturn's clouds. The swirls are violent storms just like those on Jupiter.

In 1977, *Voyager 1* and *Voyager 2* blasted off for the

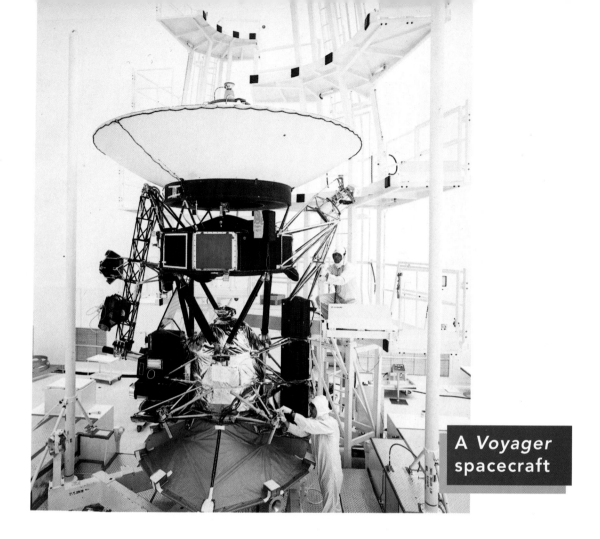

outer planets. *Voyager 1* reached Saturn in 1980. *Voyager 2* arrived less than a year later. The two *Voyager*

Many tiny ringlets make up Saturn's rings.

probes made amazing discoveries before flying on to Uranus and Neptune.

The probes found that each of Saturn's major rings is made up of thousands of ringlets, or thin rings! They also learned that Saturn has some of the strongest winds in the solar system. Near its equator, the wind roars at 1,100 miles (1,770 km) per hour. Finally, they discovered several new moons.

Spokes!

Voyager 1 sent back pictures of something astronomers had never seen before—spokes on Saturn's rings. These light and dark markings rotate like bicycle spokes around the planet along with the rings. Scientists think the markings may be dust particles, but they are not certain.

The dark markings in this photograph are "spokes" in Saturn's rings.

Saturn's Moons

Saturn has more moons than any other planet in the solar system. By 1980, scientists had discovered thirteen moons through their telescopes. Then the two *Voyager* flights found more. In 1995, the Hubble Space Telescope, a giant telescope orbiting in space, found others. So far, scientists have found twenty moons orbiting Saturn, and they think there may be still more.

Most of Saturn's moons are made of ice and rock and many have craters, or holes, on their surfaces. These craters were formed when other objects in

Saturn's moon Dione has many craters.

space crashed into the moons. Most of Saturn's moons are round, but a few have unusual shapes.

Titan is Saturn's largest moon and the second-largest moon in the solar system. Only Jupiter's moon Ganymede is larger. Although Titan is a moon, it is larger than the planets Mercury and Pluto. Scientists want to study Titan more closely because it has a thick atmosphere. This is

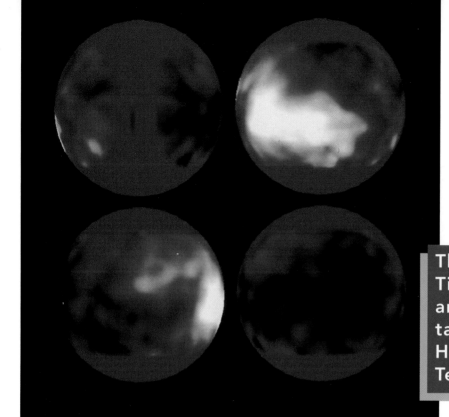

The surface of Titan from four angles, as taken by the Hubble Space Telescope

something no other moon in the solar system has. Also, Titan's atmosphere is mostly nitrogen. This makes it somewhat similar to Earth's atmosphere.

The Future

On October 15, 1997, the *Cassini Orbiter* blasted into space. It will reach Saturn in 2004.

The *Cassini Orbiter* promises to give scientists a new chance to study Titan. It will launch a probe into Titan's atmosphere shortly after it

The *Cassini Orbiter* launched in 1997.

begins to orbit Saturn. The probe, called *Huygens,* will send back information to scientists on Earth. If the probe is successful, scientists will learn more about Titan than they have ever known. While *Huygens* does its work, the *Cassini Orbiter* will be busy, too. It will orbit Saturn and send back information about this beautiful, ringed planet. Perhaps it will reveal some of the secrets that lie beneath Saturn's clouds.

The shiny probe *Huygens* is connected to the *Cassini Orbiter* (left). When it reaches Saturn (below) it will discover more secrets about the planet.

Saturn Quick Facts

Diameter	74,853 miles (120,500 km)
Average distance from the Sun	885 million miles (1.4 billion km)
Average cloud temperature	–193 degrees Fahrenheit (–125 degrees Celsius)
Length of day	10 hours 39 minutes
Length of year	29.5 Earth-years
Moons	At least 20 and possibly more

Missions to Saturn

Mission	Launch Date
Pioneer 11 (USA)	April 6, 1973
Voyager 1 (USA)	September 5, 1977
Voyager 2 (USA)	August 20, 1977
Cassini Orbiter (USA/Europe)	October 15, 1997

To Find Out More

Here are more places to learn about Saturn and other planets in space:

 **Books**

Bailey, Donna. **The Far Planets.** Steck-Vaughn Company, 1991.

Brewer, Duncan. **Saturn.** Marshall Cavendish, 1992.

Cole, Joanna. **The Magic School Bus: Lost in the Solar System.** Scholastic, Inc., 1990.

Landau, Elaine. **Saturn.** Franklin Watts, 1991.

Simon, Seymour. **Saturn.** William Morrow and Co., 1985.

Organizations and Online Sites

The Children's Museum of Indianapolis
3000 N. Meridian Street
Indianapolis, IN 46208
(317) 924-5431
http://childrensmuseum.org/sq1.htm

Visit the SpaceQuest Planetarium to see what it has to offer, including a view of this month's night sky.

National Aeronautics and Space Administration (NASA)
http://www.nasa.gov

At NASA's home page, you can access information about its exciting history and present resources and missions.

National Air and Space Museum
Smithsonian Institution
601 Independence Ave. SW
Washington, DC 20560
(202) 357-1300
http://www.nasm.si.edu/

The National Air and Space Museum site gives you up-to-date information about its programs and exhibits.

The Nine Planets
http://seds.lpl.arizona.edu/nineplanets/nineplanets/

Take a multimedia tour of the solar system and all its planets and moons.

Space Telescope Science Institute
3700 San Martin Drive
Johns Hopkins University
Homewood Campus
Baltimore, MD 21218
(410) 338-4700
http://www.stsci.edu//

The Space Telescope Science Institute operates the Hubble Space Telescope. Visit this site to see pictures of the telescope's outer-space view.

Windows to the Universe
http://windows.engin.umich.edu/

This site lets you click on all nine planets to find information about each one. It also covers many other space subjects, including important historical figures, scientists, and astronauts.

Important Words

astronomer a scientist who studies objects in space

atmosphere the gases that surround a planet

axis an imaginary line about which a planet turns

orbit to travel around an object

oxygen a gas people need to breathe

pole either end of a planet's axis

probe a spacecraft used to study space

rotate to spin

telescope an instrument that makes faraway objects look closer

Index

Meet the Author

Larry Dane Brimner was born in Florida and grew up in Alaska and California. He has worked as a waiter and a teacher, but never as an astronomer. Even so, he likes to look into the night sky and wish upon falling stars. He is a full-time writer and the author of several books for Children's Press, including *E-Mail* and *The World Wide Web*.